Love is a Mixtape

Sushmita Singh

BookLeaf Publishing

India | USA | UK

Presentation by *BookLeaf Publishing*

Web: www.bookleafpub.com

E-mail: info@bookleafpub.com

ISBN:9789360946777

First edition 2024

DEDICATION

This book is dedicated to people who are looking for words to heal and hands to hold.

Come let me walk you home!

PREFACE

As humans, loving and grieving come as naturally to us as breathing. The two universal languages that make us who we are and also bind us to one another.

As a child love was always beautiful and glorious but as I grew up things changed and so changed the meaning of love. Love became messy and chaotic. Love started to lose the easiness it carried within itself and started to be measured in the power people held over one another.
In spite of all the changes love went through in front of my eyes, the urge to see it like when I was a child never went away.

An eye for an eye has never brought us any good but somewhere deep down we know that a tree planted anywhere in the world changes everything about that place.
The soil, the air, the sky and the way everything around it starts to look.

Love is that tree!

By sharing this book of poems with you I wanted to sow that seed and I hope to give a hand, a shoulder to lean on/maybe cry and a hug to know that you are safe here and also to remind that even when we feel too much we need to keep sowing the seed and let the tree grow.

So that someday we will sit together under its blooming shade and look at the magic we could create around us with whatever we had.
I believe that is the day we will be able to see love like we were a child again.

All kinds of love

Love outgrows the clothes it was made to fit
into,

Love is nostalgia of the scribbled farewell high
school shirt,

Love is adamant and waits even when the lover
leaves,

Love knows nothing close to patience on some
days,

Love lies and expects truth,

Love steals and expects honesty,

Love hardens and expects vulnerability,

Love is random hurts and practiced apologies,

Love stays quiet when asked for answers,

Love explains when least expected,

Love is the calmness of bathroom singing,

Love never calls or texts, rather gives chances to
others to reach out,

Love takes the longest route to reach home,

Love gets lost a million times before reaching
destinations,

Love knows nothing and yet acts smart,

Love eats a lot and has an upset stomach,

Love is not good at maths but remembers dates,
times and moments like the
multiplication table of two,

Love is heartbroken, wounded yet fearless,

Love is old and fragile yet a young girl at heart.

Love is all the definitions that come to your mind

'Coz Love is handmade,
Love is grieved,
Love is flawed,
Love is human,
Love is YOU!

Poets

An awkward hello,

A stupid smile,

Many meaningless pauses,

Just completing a normal sentence takes ounces
of calculation,

Being a socially awkward person,
I think I lack the art of conversation!

Or maybe I am not someone you can/should talk
to...

Maybe I am just someone you look at like you
look at

Flowers,

Rivers

Buzzing bees,

Lovers,

Flying planes,

French doors,

Bougainvilles,

 Mountains,

And

Poets!

Temple

I know I have a thing
for sadness
but I am not a
masochist.

I am hopeful!

I am hopeful that one
day I will build a
temple and carve a
stone
in the shape of the globe
and on it in seven
billion different ways
I will write grief!

Goodbyes

One midnight I went to look for myself in the
mirror and I wasn't amazed when I couldn't find
myself,
I knew since the beginning when I had started to
lose myself,
but I wasn't aware I would be gone so soon!
The first time, I raised my hand to my head and
signalled it in a wave, I remember vapourizing a
little,

And nothing more but it even rained a little
My heart burnt
And the flames were the colour of the sky
And my dearest people that was my first
Goodbye!

This isn't a poem but a letter to tell you that life
is nothing but a long-fetched love affair
We stumble upon people and then they drift
This isn't supposed to be a tragedy but on the
way, you will find others like you
Others you can share a few words and a loud
laugh with
And that is where you will learn connections
won't happen all the time
It's as rare as a rainbow
Not every person you meet can draw you into
their mind
Learning all through the way you find,
each goodbye happened to be one of a kind!

With that said now
I saw many leave thereafter
And with each one, I went clouds
I have noticed rain more closely since then
It has always poured in these times
It wasn't the rain but me that fell
And what of me remained is vanishing like those
cattle bells!

All that's gone and going will still be treasured
and cherished
'coz there awaits a life beyond the goodbyes and
heartaches

People, places and things are meant to drift and
so, I wish for hands long enough to hold myself
on days like these!

So everyone sing it out loud,
There will be days
When it rains outside
And you will know in your heart it's time
It's time to let go of what you thought could be
kept on hold
'coz seasons change and so do people!

Associations

I can associate with the saddest things in the
world
Not just anguish and heartbreaks
But with hunger and homelessness too
'Coz hunger isn't just about food and
homelessness isn't just the absence of four
walls!

Love letter

If you ever wrote me a letter...

I would read it until the end of time,

I would read it on loop like my favourite song,

I would often take it along on long walks and
read it in the silence of the wild...
to the birds and trees,
to the clouds and breeze,
to random strangers and animals free,
I would read it to the sky!

I would sing it like a lullaby...
to grieving old souls and babies new,
to toddlers who cannot sleep in tune,
to mothers who are tired and worried,
to artists who wait for their only muse!

And for I have heard a lover's letter is a poet's
poem,
on random nights when they are breathless,
sleepless and not themselves anymore!

In a garden of Columbine and Lupine,
Aster and Wisteria,
A garden all purple and green,
I would read your letters like it is a flower
blooming in spring!

Edible grief

I read a poem with holes in it,
holes that would let me breathe through!

A poem that strains my grief like a strainer does
to the tea leaves and all that is
left, is edible grief!

Grief you can sleep over,
Grief you can talk about,
Grief you gradually learn to laugh out loud!

On those nights
to be held and heard,
a poem like this is an audience in the crowd!

Spring in my dreams

Now that I have held onto you for so long
I choose to let you go
I gift you freedom maybe not so desired at this
moment but what is needed in this hour
I gift you freedom, freedom from my mind
I want you to fly away
now like a free bird would
I don't want to keep you caged here in my heart
anymore
While I stay back and look at you walking away
I hold myself close
Close enough as my heart witnesses a sunset
inside
I burn and I burn alone
The red hues on my cheek aren't yours anymore
but 'coz of the fire inside me
Maybe I am dying a slow death

Maybe it will take some time before it swallows
me completely
Till then I am still where you left me on the
airport porch
Watching you walk away, watching you go
I have lived 52 years in a span of 28
Two days at a time, 48 hours in a go
I have held winters in my heart
I have melted summers in my eyes
I have let seasons flow through these nerves of
mine
I am an old ripped apart soul waiting for the
world to console
Or maybe I am just the drops of water on my
own forehead, mere vapours of
my own conscience
I let the vapours tickle down my own backbone
Lately, very lately I have been trying to find a
home
Home in vapours, clouds, asteroids, planets,
black holes and this universe which
shouts out loud
You are seeking things which nobody ever found
out
Silence engulfs me before death could
And I lose all my chaos, all my beauty
And the only beautiful thing I could remember is
the spaces between your
fingers

……the only home I have been seeking for so
long
Astounding as it may sound and blurred as it
may seem
I have held you like a comet in my eyes
But in the darkness of my heart, I don't say them
out loud
Instead, I smoke it out while sitting on my
backyard couch
'coz lately, very lately I have been looking for a
home
'coz lately, very lately a woman wants to sleep
'coz often, very often you awake the autumn in
my heart
and so I fold the sunrise carpet rolled out, put the
flowers in my hair to rest
and in the autumn of my heart, I let you go
and while I see you walking away, watching you
go out of sight
I slowly fell asleep
But wake me up when this autumn passes
Wake me up when October ends
Wake me up when flowers bloom
'Coz often, very often I have witnessed springs
in my dreams.

Re-creation

Like every little piece
of music that talks
about the beauty of
love,
life and longing is
being recreated
year after year,
people after people.

The same way since
time immemorial we
have been recreated
to stay in love,
with remixes of grief!

Tribe

We sing from the same flute of embarrassment
Spreading ourselves too thin
Dipped in metaphors of similarities
We love with everything we have
Me and the woman from my tribe!

There is a lot of shame we bury under our skin
to make it thick enough to abstain from any kind
of it further
Carry it around like the heavy baggage it is and
tune them in melodies of guilt
Me and the women from my tribe!

To laugh
To love
To be comfortable in our own skins
To rest
To be who we truly are
We always seek permission
Me and the women from my tribe!

Although there is a lot to wonder, why do we?

Sometimes

Sometimes grief
doesn't cry,
seek attention,
ask for a shoulder
or sit alone in a
corner.
Rather
Laughs the loudest,
Ignores blissfully,
Gives other a
shoulder and all the
love
and never lets
anybody sit in a
corner.

Seize

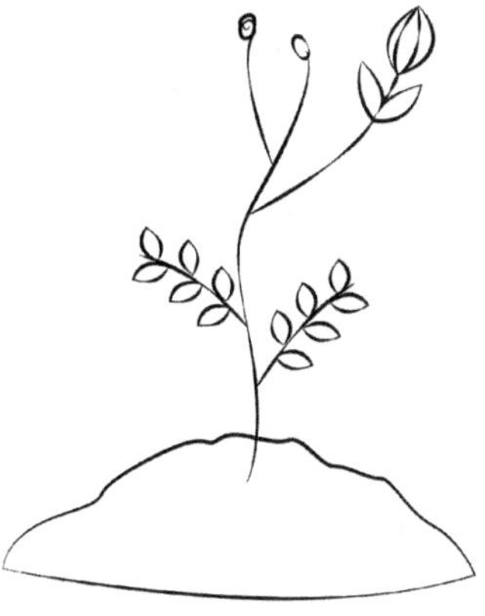

Recently grief is
consuming all the
beautiful humans

…looking into their
eyes seizing their
soul.

Did I ever tell you to
stay safe?

Fear

In the name of caste,

Colour,

Religion,

People around me
are often lynched

And

I am perturbed,

Uncomfortable,
Disturbed,

But mostly I am
scared,

What if one day I am
not?

Homecoming

Isn't that how you have always come back for
me?
Always!
I read somewhere that songs heard and people
loved, always come back!
And so I have always heard you on loop
however melancholic it got
You have changed homes and places
Places and people
People and hearts
Hearts and eyes
Eyes and souls
But somehow the nest you created on the
branches of my ribcage seems

to stay
It's tattered and the twigs are littered around but
that's what an abandoned
home looks like
That's what homes that wait for their only
person look like
Maybe now I know why Kashmir looks so
tattered and littered
Waiting has always been a thing that could rip
you apart
Or simply grow mosses and algae in your heart
Stagnant beings we go away from our homes
into rented places
Away from our people into rented hearts
I realise the pain Kashmir and I share is almost
the same
We are both waiting for our people
We are both caught up in the chaos of life we
don't want
We are both the strongest tools of politics
Kashmir is a burning place and I, a living
democracy
But we choose hope despite the despair and
prepare for a homecoming
We plan to deck the roof with stars and rainbows
And place the moon for your spotlight
When you walk back
I want you to walk back in glory like a king
would after winning battles

Till then I stand like a lonely fort in the
mountains of Kashmir growing hopes
on the branches of coniferous
And I let your words echo through this soul of
time
"I will always comeback for you"
"

… always comeback for you"
"

…… comeback for you"
"

… for you"
"

"… you"

What is Grief?

Whose grief stands taller than our own?
Nobody's!
Yes, because our grief is like our favorite child
and nobody stands superior to
them.
our grief is the utmost form of pain one can
endure and I think grief
is nothing but a measure of change!
come to think of it
when the tectonic plates shift
Aren't there earthquakes and Tsunamis?
If nature has to pay for the change, so do we as
humans.
Grief is the cost we pay for the changes!

To Die Like a Folk Song

Someone long back told me when I smile, I
remind him of the folk song his grandmother
sang every night when he was a little boy,

He went on saying that how now nobody even
remembers the words of the song and slowly
tried humming it in his not-so-melodious voice,

I look at his face and how his eyes shone in the
moment and those tears that froze at the corners
of his eyes while talking about the song,

He took pauses while humming the broken tunes
of the forgotten folk song, to swallow the lump
in his throat!
He looks at me without words but in that
moment between us, there was so much grief!

The kind of grief that takes a moment to register
the presence of all that is happening around you,
the kind that comes with the memory of
something that was loved and now stays
forgotten and buried in its own broken tunes!

In that space between us,
A desire took its root,
A desire to be hummed even by one, if
forgotten by the ton,
A desire to die like a folk song!

Colour Blue

I run to the courtyard
Stand somewhere in the middle of it
And start staring at the sky
I remember the colours, all of it
Sometimes the blue resembled the colour of the
shirt that you wore to a small gathering with
your friends,
On some days it's so white that it looks like the
cotton with which Ma often cleaned my wounds,
On some evenings I remember it was reddish
with hues of orange here and there and it was
similar to the painting behind you in one of
your photographs,
But at night it is dark and it looks like the colour
of water in deep wells

But I remember I was small and the sky was the
colour blue,
Only blue,
Warmest blue
Like the blue of Ma's banarasi saree
Neatly folded and kept into the almirah but
seldom wore,
The same blue colour was Ma's dupatta which I
saw as a piece of inheritance
She got it from her mother and I always thought
that was more mine than her

The blue colour of the sky slowly started
resonating with my soul,
And everything that was blue felt like something
I owned,
I grew up and I heard people associating blue
colour with pain and sadness
And I could feel the grief
The colour that stood as the warmest one for me
how could it be sewn with pain and not relief
Memories had it since then
And I grew a thing for sadness too!

I have too often seen you in dreams
Under the blue sky
Wearing a darker blue shirt
You looking around the snow-clad mountains
I look at you looking around

And that is when you turn
'coz turning around is love
And love is the colour blue!

Walking towards the end of
the world

The waves of longing, nostalgia and loneliness come crashing on the tips of my fingers every time your touch-inflicted memories come washing the shore of my mind!

This one amber colour memory that still glows in the darkness of your yellow-stained walls, rips my heart away in a million ways I didn't even know it existed!

The memory of your soft brown colour hands on my fading away palms and evaporating fingers.

The remembrance of a straw-thatched hut between the spaces of your long slender fingers makes me want to close my eyes and in a crowded room/street/road take a moment to

exhale the memory that otherwise would seep in
my poetries in the black of the night...and all
that would be emitted on the paper would be
caught in a cul-de-sac!

On nights when I decide to zip up all your
memories I wonder wondering you about me,
somewhere at 3 am..by the sea/on your
bed/looking through the window/smoking on
your balcony/staring at the mountains...I think
through the scenario of the world ending and on
a night that wouldn't see the next sun...you walk
towards me through the last stars of the
vanishing world!

And I don't know but, how much ever hard I try
the zip breaks and the memories never stay in a
place but are scattered all over and I like the sky
carry all of them all over me like tiny
stars...massive are the stars in real and also dead!

And however meaningless and out of tune my
words may sound to you but it helps me breathe
through the walls of time and distance that we
carry between us all the time and thinking again
through the scenario of the world crumbling
down I wonder if all that I would ever write
about
is poetries on love and you!

www.ingramcontent.com/pod-product-compliance
Lightning Source LLC
La Vergne TN
LVHW010921200726
843509LV00013B/2027